Book by Nidia Panyzza
Discover more meditations for kids & families
by visiting minibuddha.club

JOURNEY
TO THE
STARS

**Bedtime Relaxation Practices
For Kids & Families**

with real pictures of the stars
featuting talented photographers

Proofreading:
Marcela Cintra

ISBN: 978-1-7775153-3-1

www.minibuddha.club
Vancouver, Canada, 2022

Lalá,
you are a
star ☆
with love,
mom

How to use this book

My intention with this beautiful book is to support families in connecting in a peaceful and relaxing way at bedtime. These practices will help your children conquer a lovely night's sleep.

Choose one or more practices each night. Then, snuggle down and enjoy the moment.

I recommend always starting with the gratitude moment. Acknowledging the small and essential things in life is vital to accessing the stars inside our hearts.

With love,

Nidia

Are you ready for bedtime?
Did you brush your teeth?
Did you put your PJs on?

It's time to get comfy and enjoy this
relaxing and extraordinary moment.

First, let's remember the beautiful
things that happened during the day.

What are you thankful for today?

GRATITUDE
MOMENT

Being thankful makes your heart shine
bright like a star.

when you take time to appreciate life, you open your heart to receive the good from the Universe.

You acknowledge the good and receive more and more good things from the same source - an unlimited source of love and light!

So, close your eyes and appreciate your life.

Be thankful for family, your mom, dad, or the person who takes care of you.

Be thankful for the school, your food, the cozy bed.

Be thankful for being alive, for breathing, and for being loved.

Close your eyes and let your heart feel the power of gratitude. How beautiful is your life? How amazing are the small things around you?

MINDFUL
BREATHING

Breathing is your magic power; it's an
effortless and beautiful space where you
can cultivate true inner calm.

Sit down comfortably or lay down on your bed. Invite your attention to your breath. Notice how each breath moves in and out of your body quite effortlessly.

What do you *feel* when the air comes through your nose? Is that cold? Warm? Do you notice anything different?

There is a powerful source of beautiful energy that helps you breathe. So, you don't need to change your natural breathing rhythm - just notice it.

As you breathe, observe the pause at the end of each exhale.

Feel your chest gently expanding and relaxing. Witness the air moving through your nose, throat and chest (and back out again).

BODY SCAN

RELAXATION

Your little body is the safest place to be—
the house of your soul.

Take a few minutes to observe each part of your body, from your toes up to the top of your head.

Lay down on your bed and take a deep and relaxing breath. Let your body cozy up and relax.

Do you feel your face? Can you feel your hands? Each of your fingers? Even your nails?

As you pay attention to each body part, gently relax that area. While noticing your neck, relax the neck! While paying attention to your shoulders, try to soften them.

RELAXING
VISUALISATION

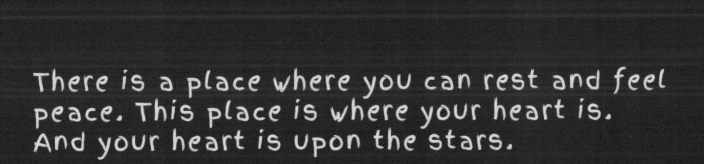

There is a place where you can rest and feel peace. This place is where your heart is. And your heart is upon the stars.

Choose a cozy spot in your bed and close your eyes.
Use your imagination to picture a place in nature
that *feels* relaxing and happy to you.

It can be that green park close to your house, a bright
sunny beach, a mountain or a lake. Imagine yourself
close to nature and take a deep breath.

Try to identify the smells and notice the colors.
What is it like to be close to the trees? Can you hear
the little birds singing around?

You can not only hear the sounds but also see, and
feel everything around you.
Everything is so real, so rich.

As your imagination brings you to the most stunning
places on earth, you start acknowledging you have all
the beauty inside your heart.

PEACEFUL

OUTER SPACE

You, your house, family, friends and,
everything around you are a peaceful haven
full of sparkling stars.

Close your eyes and cover them with your little hands. Feel the warmth of your hands touching your eyelids, and breathe.

Notice your thought space is empty. You can visualise your own outer space. Suddenly, with your intention, you can see a beautiful sky full of stars.

Then imagine that the stars are starting to shine brighter and brighter and that the lights from the stars touch your heart. Your entire being and thoughts are so serene and calming that you may fall asleep now.

Feel that you are part of this big and beautiful universe of yours. Feel you are such a star!

SELF-LOVE

MEDITATION

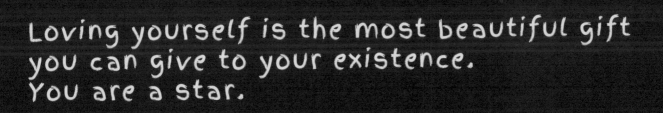

Loving yourself is the most beautiful gift
you can give to your existence.
You are a star.

Sit down or lay down and relax.
Hands to heart.

Take a moment to perceive the beautiful
person you are.

Remind yourself you are special, you are
unique, you are intelligent and creative.

You are made of stardust. You are bright,
energetic and perfect. You are everything you
want to be.

Say out loud:

I am special
I am unique
I am intelligent
I am creative

Say out loud:

I love myself
I am love
I am loved

Repeat 3 x while breathing slowly.

BREATHING

WALTZ

You are deeply fulfilled by the energy and light of the stars. As you breathe, you can feel the power within your heart.

Calm down. Your beautiful journey to the stars is about to start. All you need to do is enjoy this lovely and quiet moment of the day.

So sit down on your bed or your favorite spot in the house, take a deep breath and prepare to start counting.

Inhale for 4 counts, hold the breath for 4 counts, exhale for 4 counts, pause and repeat. You can continue using this relaxing breathing meditation for about 10 times or as long as you like.

Thank you to the beautiful and talented photographers
featured in this book - without you, this book would not
be the same.

Cover: Photo by Bess Hamiti
For Lalá: photo by Nikita Grishin
Ready for bedtime: photo by Wendy Wei
Gratitude moment: photo by Eberhard Grossgasteiger
Mindful breathing: photo by Felipe Helfstein
Body scan relaxation: photo by Faik Akmd
Relaxing visualization: photo by Neale LaSalle
Peaceful outer space: photo by Adam Krypel
Self-love meditation: Photo by Helena Lopes
Breathing waltz: photo by Bess Hamiti
This page: photo by Julia
You are made of stardust: photo by Dids

You are
made of
Stardust ☆

ABOUT THE AUTHOR

Nidia, Lalá & Benja

Hi, my name is Nidia and these are Lavinia, my daughter and Benjamin, my fur baby.

My mission is to guide kids & their families to start practicing meditation and relaxation in a simple and friendly way.

Taking time to relax, take deep breaths and acknowledge the good things in life are essential to build a healthy and beautiful relationship with our kids. Enjoy these moments with your little ones and see how peaceful (or more peaceful) your nights and life can be.

with love, ★

Nidia

www.minibuddha.club

CPSIA information can be obtained
at www.ICGtesting.com
Printed in the USA
LVHW071945101022
730379LV00008B/147